Nintendo Labo Kit for Switch: The Unofficial Guide to Getting Started, Using, & Building

Copyright 2018 by HSE Guides
Third Edition, License Notes

Copyright Info:

This book is intended for personal reference material only. This book is not to be re-sold or redistributed to individuals without the consent of the copyright owner. If you did not pay for this book or have obtained it through illicit means then please purchase an authorized copy online. Thank you for respecting the hard work of this author.

Legal Info:

This book in no way, is affiliated or associated by the Original Copyright Owner, nor has it been certified or reviewed by the party. This is an un-official/non-official book. This book does not modify or alter the game and is not a software program.

Presented by
HiddenStuffEntertainment.com

Table of Contents

Preface

We want to take a moment to say thank you for purchasing our strategy guide online. HiddenStuff Entertainment remains one of the top app and eBook publishers online. It is our commitment to bring you the latest support and strategies for today's most popular games.

We sincerely hope that you find this guide useful and beneficial in your quest for digital immortality. We want to provide gamers with knowledge and build their skills to perform at the highest levels within their games. This in turn contributes to a positive and more enjoyable experience. After all, it is our belief that things in life are to be enjoyed as much as they possibly can be.

If you are in need of additional support or resources in regards to this guide, please feel free to visit our webpage at Hiddenstuffentertainment.com

FREE GAME GUIDES, TIPS, & EBOOKS

Looking for the most up to date strategies for the latest games? Sign-up for free to get these delivered straight to your inbox! Hundreds of the most recent & popular games are covered!

Click or visit the URL below to get started.

*Signup from the homepage popup or click the "newsletter" link at the top of the page.

http://www.hiddenstuffentertainment.com/

Introduction

"I want to dominate this game!"

You probably already well know the feeling of crushing your opponent, getting that rare item, gathering lots of resources and becoming rich, or perhaps that moment when you finally triumph and beat the game!

Of course, for all of us this is often a path of anguish, frustration, and often a dream that is given up on too early. Such is, the nature of the video games we play today.

Are you feeling as if no matter what you do, you are unable to beat certain parts of the game?

This is where we come to help! Gathering the most seasoned players and authors from across the globe we continually help gamers just like you achieve all the feats the game has to offer. Whether you are a new player or a seasoned veteran, we guarantee you will always be surprised with the strategies, tips, walkthroughs, cheats, and guidance that we provide.

Enjoying a game to its fullest and being happy with the experience is no longer a dream. With this guide, it's a reality.

With this eBook you will learn how to:
- Dominate your opponents.
- Beat the game.
- Get the best items.
- Walkthroughs to guide you through the game.
- Tips, tricks, and strategies from the pros.
- And so much more!

We wrote this book because we want to help you become the very best in your game. We want you to enjoy it as much as possible. And we want you to have the success that few pro players have enjoyed. By following their strategies you too can have all this and more.

Read on to learn how to dominate the game!

Getting Started

This game has finally been released allowing players to get various cardboard collections built. These will get your switch interacted with in a way that is fun. However, before even starting to get that giant robot backpack, piano, house, or RC car built, there are actually some things that you need to be aware of so as to get the most from your adventure in this game. If you are trying to get started, ensure that the tips below are followed.

What Does Nintendo Labo Entail?

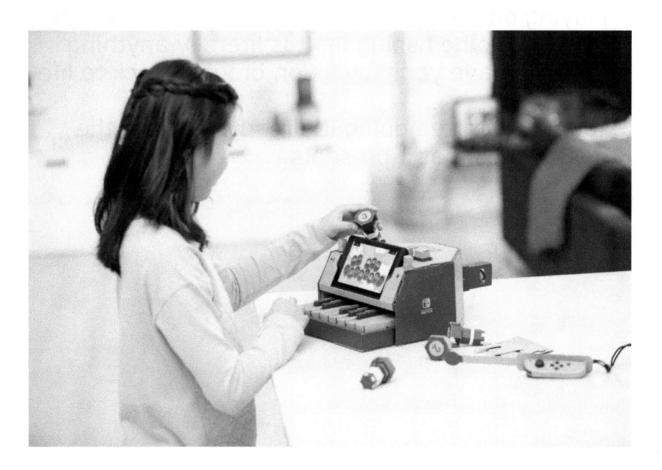

This is a group of cardboard kits that can have your switch turned into different types of objects. They are referred to as toy – con. When it comes to how many objects that your switch can be turned into, the sky is actually your limit. This happens to be the solution of Nintendo to VR and AR. There are piano keys, fishing rod, motorcycle handles, and others being made from the cardboard and also the digital screen of the switch getting combined into one package.

In practice, there is going to be a road to be driven down being displayed by the screen. The same can be said of the notes which you are playing on the piano as well as whichever water you tend to be fishing in. It is literally anything that can have your Toy – Con brought back to life.

You have started doing it already. Imagine the possibilities that it presents.

How Nintendo Labo Works

Once Nintendo Labo has been purchased as well as received, the first thing to do is have every Toy – Con arranged. The instructions for assembling are going to be displayed on the screen (switch) on 3D. This is most especially once the included application gets popped in the console. Just have the instructions followed so as to get these devices created. If you want the steps to be fast – forwarded or rewound at your pace, such is possible.

Once it has been assembled, there are lots of minigames which can be played using every Toy – Con. This is usually by having your Joy – Cons attached and then getting the supporting application opened. Basic games are what the play section is going to be kicking off with. However, you will get deeper in such experiences through the option which says Discover. The truth is that once every Toy – Con has been made, there is going to be lots of gameplay being offered.

Has There Been The Announcement of Any Toy – Con?
The answer is yes as Nintendo has been able to the following announced.

Toy Types

Toy – Con RC Car

Get Joy – Cons slotted into this cardboard. The touchscreen can be made use of in getting it moved around the house. HD rumble feature is what RC car makes use of in every Joy – Con that is to be moved.

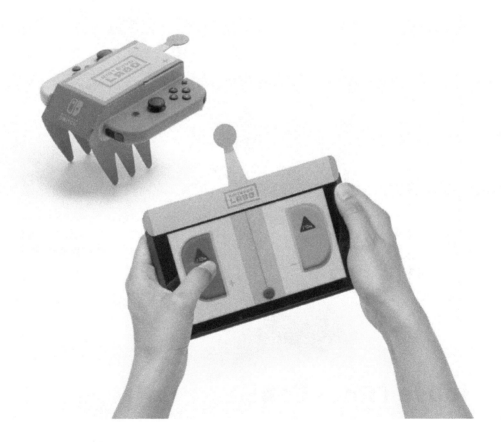

Fishing Rod (Toy - Con)

This includes cradle, string, reel and fishing rod which can be made use of in having fishing experience reproduced inside your home. Get your rod cast in the digital waters. This will enable you get hold of different exotic fish. You will get them eventually reeled in.

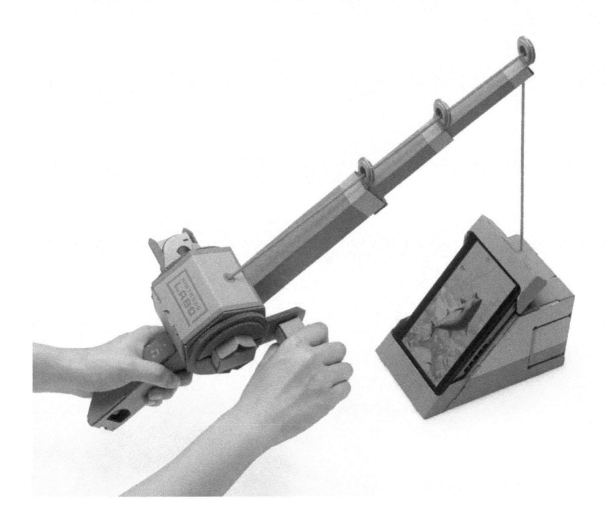

House (Toy - Con)

This actually happens to be a dolls house and cardboard is what it is made out from. Get your

switch slotted in the opening after which you will be interacting with the creature which is cute inside. There are also various blocks that you can get access to. You will need to get these slotted on the sides for the purpose of playing games with them, feeding, and also having to interact with those pets of yours that are new.

Motorbike (Toy - Con)

This includes, ignition, throttle and group of handles just like what you have got in real life. Motion controls are what you use in turning. If you want to pass through corners that are sharp then you may need to lean genuinely.

Piano (Toy - Con)

This is actually a cardboard piano that has thirteen keys. Every key has been attached to a strip (reflective). This is what enables the IR

sensor inside the Joy – Con (right) uses in sensing the key which has been pressed. This is what will ensure that music gets created on the display of switch. It possible to have different types of knob assembled in other to get different notes and sound effects created.

Robot (Toy - Con)

This will have you turned into Godzilla and is a
suit which is wearable. It comes with backpack as
well as visor which you do play in various

minigames as switch gets docked to the television.

FAQ

Can Toy – Con Be Purchased Individually?
Unfortunately, no. Every Toy – Con which has so far been announced have been included inside the initial or first pack. On the 20th and 27th of April, it is going to be launched in Europe and north America respectively. Toy – Con happens to be the only exception. This is because it is sold separately.

Do They Sell Nintendo Labo In Packs?
The answer is yes. They are being referred to as kits though. Different kit includes Piano, motorbike, house, fishing rod and RC Car. Robot is only what the Robot kit contains.

How Can Nintendo Lab Kit Be Gotten?

Nintendo Labo can be purchased online from Nintendo store. You can also get it from participating retailers. Details haven't been released just yet. However, it is possible to make a pre – order today from Amazon. There are toy shops that you can get this from in the nearest future.

Best Tips

Time And Space Should Be Set Aside

This game is a do it yourself project and as such, needs your time a lot. Apart from the RC car, majority of the Toy – Cons which you will be getting built are going to take about 1 – 4 hours. This is why planning is very essential. Also, ensure that the surface which you want to make use of in building are actually large and clean. These cardboard sheets are going to get your workspace filled up very fast.

There Should Be A Garbage Can

As your cardboard cutouts get folded into toys that are playable, there is going to be some craps which will come from having to get holes punched out. There should be something to ensure that such an area is clutter free.

Fold Lines Should Always Be Increased

Whenever you start working on a cardboard piece that is new, the application or software will want you to have all the fold lines increased. This is very important since it will ensure that the laps for every piece as well as tap are going to be interlocking perfectly as things start getting folded together.

Camera Controls Should Be Utilized

A major feature of this application has been the ability to a get a 3D view which is highly interactive. This will ensure that steps are being nailed in projects you seem to be undertaking. Always remember that it is possible for you to pinch in other to zoom. You only need to get your 2 fingers spread on the screen. If you want to rotate, one finger should be moved. If you want

to move from one side to another, the 2 fingers should be slided at once.

Also, if you want to go through some sets of instructions after going ahead, get the forward icon slided to the screen's right.

Tabletop Mode Tends To Be The Best (Docked Mode Does Work Very Well)

Since you are going to be interacting with lots of instructions, the best thing is to get your switch propped up in tabletop mode in the building process. It is also possible to make use of a Labo application with the switch being docked to a

television. The interface of Labo is actually very compatible with controllers. It is possible to make use of additional joy cons or a pro controller for some games like RC car.

Your Switch Should Always Be Charged

Ensure that your switch gets plugged as the game goes on since you will be using Labo to work for some hours. If you want to charge and play, dock mode option is what you should make use of. You can also get a switch stand picked up. This could be Hori's $13 Compact Playstand and can help you remain in tabletop mode just as you charge.

Labo App Is Going To Ensure That Your Progress Is Saved
Every progress that you have made is being saved by the application. This will enable you to start from any point which you have stopped. Also, if you want to know whether you are almost getting a building finished, you can make use of the icon which is at the screen's bottom right. As the circle is getting closer to being filled, that is how your building is close to being completed.

RC Car Has Got A Camera Mode That Is Hidden

The first thing that you will need to get built once you have access to Labo variety kit is the RC Car. The circular button should be pressed in the screen's center as the RC car is being controlled in play mode. An interface that is new is going to be opened up through which you will be able to get the car's speed adjusted. In the center, there is a camera feed which taps into the IR blaster of Joy – Cons. It should be tapped so as to have thermal camera modes and night vision alternated.

Hidden Builds Can Be Unlocked

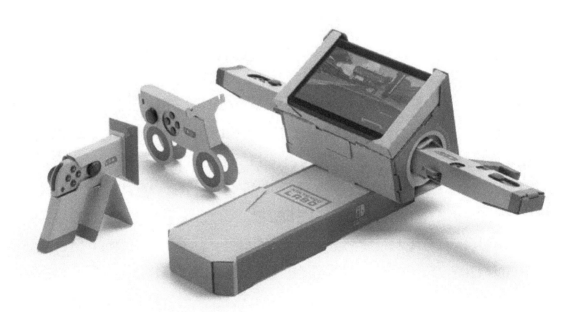

It has been stated that the Labo variety kit contains 5 Toy – Con. These are fishing rod,

piano, RC car, motorbike, and house.However, it may interest you to know that there are more. There are 2 mini builds that you will discover as soon as you begin to get motorbike Toy – Con worked on. These are Toy-Con mini-bike and Toy-Con scanner.

Replacement Parts Can Be Ordered For

If it happens that your cardboard creations got destroyed for one reason or the other, there is no need to panic. This is because Nintendo has made it possible that parts can be ordered online. Since the software can't be gotten separately, this is really perfect.

Conclusion

Once you start to implement the strategies outlined there will be enjoying your new Nintendo Labo kit in not time. In addition, you will find yourself secrets which you never knew existed. This will not only make the game much more interesting and enjoyable but you will also realize a greater level of accomplishment. Good luck!